For The Animals

TOD

Wagging Tales

*Conversations with
Our Animal Friends*

Every Animal Has a Tale

Tim Link

EMERALD
BOOK CO.

Published by Emerald Book Company
Austin, TX
www.emeraldbookcompany.com

Distributed by Emerald Book Company

For ordering information or special discounts for bulk purchases, please contact Emerald Book Company at PO Box 91869, Austin, TX 78709, 512.891.6100.

Design and composition by Greenleaf Book Group LLC
Cover design by Greenleaf Book Group LLC

Publisher's Cataloging-In-Publication Data
(Prepared by The Donohue Group, Inc.)

Link, Tim, 1964-
   Wagging tales : every animal has a tale : conversations with our animal friends / by Tim Link.
-- 1st ed.

   p. : ill. ; cm.

   ISBN: 978-1-934572-14-6

1. Human-animal communication--Anecdotes. I. Title.

QL776 .L56 2009
591.59   2009920751

Part of the Tree Neutral™ program, which offsets the number of trees consumed in the production and printing of this book by taking proactive steps, such as planting trees in direct proportion to the number of trees used: www.treeneutral.com

Printed in the United States of America on acid-free paper

09 10 11 12 13 14   10 9 8 7 6 5 4 3 2 1

First Edition

TreeNeutral

Dedication

To all of the beautiful animals who opened up their hearts and told me their stories. To all of my friends and family who have supported me on this wonderful journey. To my wonderful wife, Kim, who is my inspiration in all that I do. To my precious furry boys, Buzz and Woody, who were my muses in writing this book. To Spirit, for giving me this wonderful gift of being able to communicate with the animals and give them a voice. Thank you, God! Thank you, God!

Contents

Preface

You may ask, what is animal communication? The broad definition of animal communication is the ability to communicate telepathically with animals of all types. It is sometimes referred to as interspecies communication as well.

For me, this involves establishing a telepathic connection with the animal either by being in the proximity of the animal or through the use of a picture of the animal. Once a connection is made, I communicate to the animal any questions its human companion(s) may have. I then provide the response I receive from the animal to its human companion.

The information an animal conveys to me can come in the way of images, smells, tastes, words, or feelings. Images may be communicated to show me the animal's surroundings. Odors may be communicated so that I can tell the human companion what smells may be offensive or causing an allergic reaction (e.g., chemicals, perfumes, cigarette smoke, etc.). Tastes may be communicated to me so that I can convey if a medicine is leaving an unusual taste in the animal's mouth. Words are communicated to me so that I can convey the exact words the animal wants to say to its human companion. Finally, sometimes animals will share their feelings with me, such as happiness or dislike, or maybe they feel ill or are experiencing physical discomfort.

Some animals can be very communicative and others are not. However, I have yet to encounter an animal that has declined my request to communicate with it on behalf of its human companion. In fact, most welcome it as a way to let their human companions know what their preferences are or if they are not feeling well.

Introduction

Ibet you are wondering how someone becomes an animal communicator. For some, the ability presents itself early in their lives. After all, we each have the ability to speak to one another and to our animals telepathically. When we are very young, this seems very normal. Most of us have spent time talking to the animals in our lives. We have communicated with them either through spoken words or through a telepathic connection. Unfortunately, when we get to be about five or six years old, we tend to lose this ability. We start to rely more on the spoken word, and we are taught that this is the only way to communicate. Thus, we suppress our inherent telepathic abilities and cease to further develop this gift. Most are never given a second chance to fully develop this gift and use it to better the world. For me, my gift presented itself at the right time in my life. I was on the right path mentally, emotionally, and spiritually to accept my gift and fully develop it. It has taken me more than forty years to find my true path in life. The gift of working with and understanding animals is a true blessing.

My journey to uncovering my ability began in an unexpected way. Because my wife comes from a family of intuitive individuals on her mother's side, she often wondered if she might be able to communicate with animals. So, for her birthday present, we attended an all-day workshop about learning how to communicate with animals. The workshop included meditation techniques, self-hypnosis, and practicing the technique of receiving information rather than just sending information to the animals that we worked with.

During the all-day workshop, I began to notice that I was receiving accurate information from the animals that were brought to the workshop as well as some that we worked with through pictures. Of course my first reaction was, "Am I really 'hearing' what the animal is communicating, or is this something else?" When participants of the workshop repeatedly confirmed that the information I received from the animals was accurate, I knew I must have opened a door to a very special gift.

Over the next several months, I used my newly discovered gift to communicate with my own pets and the pets of friends and family. As my confidence in my ability to communicate with animals continued to grow, I began helping others within my church with their pets as well as working with animals at the local animal rescue shelters.

My gift continues to expand on a daily basis. An example of this is that in the beginning, I needed a picture of the animal in order to establish a communication connection with it. Now, I can communicate with the animal by simply speaking with its human companions either by phone or in person.

It is truly a blessing to help bridge the communication gap between animals and their human companions. I believe that this is my true purpose for being here, and I thoroughly enjoy each opportunity I am given to further that purpose.

The following are some of the tales the animals have shared with me. The tales are funny, heartfelt, intriguing, and always interesting. I hope you enjoy reading about their tales as much as I have enjoyed writing about them. Remember, every animal has a tale.

If you have to relinquish your pet for any reason, fully explain to it the reason for doing this and that you won't be coming back for it. This will prevent many of the behavioral problems (guilt associated with thinking that it did something wrong, becoming withdrawn, becoming aggressive, etc.) that can surface in animals left at a shelter or with a new family without any explanation.

SPECIAL, MARMY,
CUPID, TAWNY

The Gang Finds a New Home

Our local animal rescue shelter had a family of four cats that were adopted by one family. This is not typical. Usually, one cat is adopted or possibly two at the same time, but rarely more. Because these cats had been residents of the shelter for more than two years and it was the only home they had ever known, everyone at the shelter thought it would be best to keep them together when it came time for them to be adopted. When the cats arrived at their new home, Special and Marmy seemed to adapt easily. Cupid and Tawny, however, were very leery about their new surroundings and spent most of the time hiding.

The family contacted me and asked if I could speak with all four cats. They wanted me to tell the cats that there was no reason for them to be afraid and that this was going to be their forever home. In addition, the family asked me to communicate specifically with Special to help correct a behavioral issue they were having with her.

I began the session with Tawny by asking her if I had permission to speak with her. She agreed. I asked her why she was hiding under the couch. She said, "Noises, different noises." She gave me a vision of a television and the sounds she heard from the television. Their new human companions said the television was never turned up loud and was located in another room. However, since Tawny's only home up to this point had been the shelter, she was not familiar with the sounds of a television, the occasional loud cries of her human companions' grandchildren, or some of the other household noises. I explained to Tawny that her new home had different noises from the shelter but that she shouldn't be afraid. She reluctantly accepted my advice and explained that she was hiding because she still felt unsure of her new surroundings and new family. However, she agreed to come out more often, but only when she was ready. As she put it, "My time." About five minutes later, she came out to join Marmy and Special.

During our conversation, Tawny stressed that she likes "High." She showed me a vision of a carpeted, tan cat condo (climbing post with a high perch) that she would like to have in a separate room or quiet place in the new home.

I then spoke with Cupid about why he was hiding from everyone. He said, "What Tawny does, I do." So, I told the family to watch for Cupid to start exploring more once Tawny felt more comfortable. Cupid didn't have much else to say.

Next, I asked Marmy how she was and she said, "Fine." I asked if she liked her new home and family, and she said, "Yes, I rule." She indicated to me that she felt like the leader of the group. I asked if she knew why Tawny and Cupid were hiding. She said, "Those cats? They're always hiding . . . still scared." I asked her if she would talk to them and show them that there was nothing to be scared of. She said, "Yes, of course."

I then spoke to Special, and she was the most talkative of the bunch. She showed me a tree inside the house and said, "Tree different." I asked her how the tree was different and different compared to what. She showed me the couch that Tawny and Cupid were hiding under. She showed me the tan, brown, and burgundy colors of the couch. I tried to confirm the colors with the family, but they told me the couch upholstery didn't have any of those colors in it and that it was currently covered with quilts, which one of the cats had recently urinated on. (Needless to say, none of the cats admitted to that deed.) I asked Special again about the colors of the couch, and she insisted that the couch was tan, brown, and burgundy. After further thought, the family member I was speaking with recalled that the couch had flowers that were those same colors. Special then showed me a picture window behind the couch.

I confirmed the existence of the window with the family and asked if Special or any of the cats had been up in the window or on the back of the couch. I was told that they couldn't get up in the window, and that they hadn't been seen on the back of the couch, but there was no guarantee that they hadn't been there. Special then showed me a small tree near the window and said, "Tree different." I asked again if there was a tree in the house or perhaps a banana tree. After more thought, the family member stated that there was a fake tree in the house. I asked if the tree was in the same room as the couch and if it was located in the corner of the room. She answered yes to both questions. Special then stated that she liked the different tree.

I then asked Special about the behavioral issue that the family was having with her. They did not want her to get up on the kitchen counters and dining room table. The family was afraid that Special would hurt herself or knock something off and hurt one of the other cats. I reminded her that she had already knocked some noodles off the counter and onto the floor. I asked her if she would please stay off the counters and table. She told me it was "Fun." I told her that I understood it was fun, but she needed to stay down because she might hurt herself or one of the other cats.

Special then stated, "Did before." She was referring to having free reign of her room at the shelter where she was able to climb on any of the shelves that she wanted. I explained to her that this was not her room at the shelter, and she would have to abide by the wishes of her new family. However, she could have free reign of the entire house otherwise. Special reluctantly agreed to stay down by saying in a very sarcastic tone, "Okay." I conveyed to the family that I couldn't guarantee that Special would keep to her word immediately and that she may need to be reminded to stay down. However, over time, I felt that she would comply with their wishes.

Special then showed me that she likes to look up on top of things to see what is located in the highest places. She showed me the top of the refrigerator, and she was wondering what, if anything, was on top. I asked if there were items on top of the refrigerator, and a family member said that there were three boxes with items in them. Special was interested in seeing the boxes, but she was not necessarily interested in seeing what was inside them. She then showed me that there were a lot of things on the front of the refrigerator, and conveyed that she was interested in them. It was confirmed that there were magnets and other items posted on the front of the refrigerator.

Special then showed me a picture of a cat or cats on the refrigerator; I couldn't determine whether there were one or more cats in the picture. I asked the woman if they had previously had a cat and was told that they hadn't, but that her boyfriend had. I asked if he had a picture of his previous cat on display, and she said no. After some more thought, I realized what Special was trying to tell me. She wanted her picture to be posted high up on the front of the refrigerator.

The family then told me about something they were experiencing in their house that was totally unrelated to any of the four cats. Though the house was newly built and they were the first owners, they believed they had a ghost, because they had felt the presence of a child in the attic. On more than one occasion, they felt that they had had supernatural experiences: They had found one of the upstairs doors open, even though they always keep the doors closed. The television channels had changed without anyone touching the television or the remote control. And once, one of the grandchildren had been walking up the stairs, and as she approached the landing, they heard her say, "Hello," as if she had seen someone. When they asked the grandchild whom she had been talking to, she said, "The little girl." They believe the ghost is a little girl, and they have named her Sarah. Fortunately, the ghost seems to want to play and not cause any trouble.

After they told me this story, they asked if I had the ability to communicate with ghosts. I replied that I had not had the opportunity to use my gift to communicate with humans on the other side. At that point, I had only communicated with living animals or animals that had transitioned out of our physical world. One family member asked if I could ask one of the cats if they had seen the ghost. I wasn't sure what kind of response I would get, but I decided to try. I first asked Marmy if she had seen the little girl. Marmy said, "I haven't," so then I turned to Tawny, and she stated, "Not there." At first, I wasn't sure if Tawny meant that there wasn't a little girl ghost in the house or that the ghost wasn't there at the moment. The woman then told me that Tawny had walked up the stairs, briefly looked around, and then turned around and came back down at the precise moment I was communicating with her.

I will leave you to your own conclusions as to whether or not a little girl's ghostly presence exists in the house. However, I have heard many times that children under the age of six and animals are more aware of unseen presences. Unfortunately, after the age of six, most children are usually taught to suppress their natural intuitive abilities due to the social pressures to be "normal."

I finished our conversation by asking each of the cats if they had anything else to ask or tell me. They declined any further conversation at that time.

I told the family I hoped that I had helped them and the kitties. They said I had helped and that they were pleased with what they had learned.

I suggested they consider adding more toys, a few kitty condos, and other items to stimulate the cats and to keep them active. I also suggested separate feeding dishes and litter boxes since animals typically like to have their own things.

I later found out that Tawny and Cupid were returned to the shelter a couple of weeks later because they had not adapted readily enough to their new home, and the family didn't think they were happy being there. It is my belief, after rescuing several animals during my lifetime, that it takes time, support, and a lot of love for animals to get used to their new environment. The good news is that the two cats are doing better since being returned to the shelter. This may be due in part to the familiarity of their surroundings.

GABBY

What's That Smell?

Gabby is one of the cats being cared for at our local rescue shelter. She is a spirited golden tabby with gorgeous light green eyes.

Recently Gabby was acting a little peculiar and less responsive than usual. Staff at the shelter asked me to have a conversation with her. I began by asking Gabby if I could speak with her. She said, "Of course. I remember you from your last visit."

I asked Gabby, "What's wrong? Are you feeling all right?" Gabby said, "Different room," "It smells," and "Cats looking at me." I asked Gabby if she had been moved to a different room and she said, "Yes." I asked, "Which room do you like the best?" She showed me a room that had pink walls. I later confirmed that the room with pink walls was the room that Gabby had lived in first. I asked Gabby if she would like to be moved back to the pink room and she said, "Yes."

I told the volunteer this information, and she promptly moved Gabby to a different room, but not the pink one. I visited Gabby at the shelter a week later. She was back to her spirited self and climbing the screened doors that are located at the entrance of each of the cat rooms. I asked, "How are you doing, Gabby?" She replied, "Much better, but the pink room is better."

The shelter volunteers also uncovered the "smell" that Gabby was referring to. The shelter had recently switched the type of litter being used in the litter boxes. The litter did not absorb or clump like the previous litter. Thus, the urine settled in the bottom of each tray, making it smell worse.

I have visited the shelter numerous times and have sat in each of the four cat rooms. However, I had never noticed that each room has a specific color. Animals are definitely more in tune with their environments and surroundings compared to us humans. Perhaps you can also blame my lack of noticing these types of details on my being a guy!

MELLOW, SHADY

Chasing Shady

Shady, a beautiful, solid-white cat, had been found as a stray in a local neighborhood, where a resident had been feeding him for a few weeks. The resident noticed Shady was getting thinner and had a serious neck injury from a fight with another animal. The resident called the local rescue shelter and, upon his capture, Shady was taken to the vet for a checkup. It was immediately obvious that his condition was serious enough that he would not have survived much longer on his own. Through testing, the vet discovered that Shady had FIV, a feline form of the HIV virus found in humans. FIV can be fatal for cats, but if it's treated, the cat can live a long life.

One evening when I visited the foster home where Shady had been taken to recover from his injuries, I was told that Shady had been acting timid and that he wasn't eating very much. The foster asked me to communicate with Shady to find out what he could tell me about where he came from, how he got sick, and if he needed anything.

I asked Shady if I could speak with him, and he very openly said, "Yes." I asked him if he felt okay and why was he being so timid. He said, "I'm fine, but I'm not sure where I am." I let Shady know what had happened and why he was staying in this particular home. I assured him that he was going to be okay and that we were working on finding him a good forever home. He seemed to accept my comments and immediately began to eat his food.

I next asked Shady if he would share his prior history with me and if he could tell me how he got sick. Specifically, I asked how he ended up as a stray in the neighborhood where he was found and why he had chosen the particular lady who had been feeding him. He explained that his previous family had recently moved from that neighborhood and had decided to leave him behind. He then got sick and had nowhere to go. He did not seem upset because he said, "It's fine . . . it was time." He felt that his mission had been accomplished with that family and that it was time for him to help a new family. He said he had chosen the lady from his original neighborhood to feed him because, "She is supposed to adopt me."

Interestingly enough, the lady did express to the foster that she had an interest in adopting Shady and his roommate, Mellow, another rescued cat that was sharing the same room. Ironically, the cat that she had previously owned was also FIV positive. This seemed at first to be a great match for both Shady and Mellow. However, she also said she would be declawing both cats because she didn't want them to tear up her furniture. In light of this, the foster decided not to allow the lady to adopt either cat because declawing cats went against the rescue shelter's policies for adoption.

I always enjoy my conversations with animals. I find them quite exciting, intriguing, and fun. Little did I know, the fun with Shady had just begun.

While I continued to communicate with Shady that evening, the door to his crate was left open in order for the foster to clean up his litter box, which was inside the crate. After our conversation, Shady became more comfortable with the new people in his life and his new temporary home located in one of the basement rooms of the house. Perhaps Shady had become a little too comfortable. While no one was looking, he jumped from the table where his crate was located, took a little stroll around the room, and met Mellow face-to-face. Of course, if you know cats like I do, a leisurely stroll can turn into an all-night affair.

After a short time allowing him to explore his new environment and meet Mellow, we decided it was time for him to get back into his crate. Should be easy, right? Wrong! Have you ever tried to get a cat to do something on your terms? We spent two hours chasing, cornering, and coaxing Shady back into his crate, which was not an easy task in a basement full of crawl spaces, ductwork, and fabulous hiding spaces. A word to the wise: always close the door to the crate when you don't want the animal wandering around at will unless you have a couple of hours to kill.

I had the pleasure of visiting with Shady about a month later at the same foster home. He looked really healthy and was adjusting well to his surroundings. He immediately ran over to me, no longer timid and unsure. He and Mellow had free reign of their section of the basement. I asked him how he was, and he said, "Much better." He was definitely in a very happy place and feeling really good. It just goes to show you that love cures all. Never give up on these beautiful creatures.

FRAZIER

Run Frazier Run

Frazier is a large Plott Hound mix at the local shelter. If you know anything about Plott Hounds, you know they love to run. You're probably thinking all dogs love to run, and you are correct. But Plott Hounds *really* love to run. They will run all day if you let them, and they often don't know when to stop. They love to run by themselves in open fields, but they can also be great jogging partners for their human companions.

One volunteer at the shelter loved to jog. He would visit the shelter regularly and spend a lot of time with Frazier. Frazier loved the visits and enjoyed being with the volunteer. The relationship grew, and the volunteer decided to adopt Frazier and take him home. It seemed to be an ideal situation. Both enjoyed jogging and spending time together. As a bonus for Frazier, it was a single-pet home.

The volunteer continued the same day-to-day routine he had before Frazier came to live with him, but he also began a new job. Hours left alone in his new home while his human companion was away, in addition to the visitors who occasionally stopped by, made Frazier very anxious. To his human companion, he seemed to have become aggressive since he was adopted. This behavior was not typical of Frazier, and it was more than his new human companion was prepared for, so he thought it would be best to return Frazier to the shelter.

Once he had been returned to the shelter, I asked Frazier if we could have a conversation. He was very open to the idea and wanted to tell his side of the story. I asked him what had happened at the new home and why he had changed his behavior. He said, "Not running . . . changed/changes." I asked him what had changed, and he kept repeating, "Not running . . . changed/changes." I concluded from our conversation that Frazier had not adapted well to his new home because he did not like to be left alone, or because he and his new owner didn't run as often as they had in the past.

Despite all of this, he still felt that the person who had previously adopted him was the right person. He kept repeating to me, "One . . . the one." I explained to him that sometimes relationships don't work out the way we want them to and that we must move on. I told him he was a good boy, and we would find him a perfect place to live. In the meantime, he would always have a home at the shelter, and they would take good care of him. He seemed depressed about this conclusion but was willing to accept it. I thanked him for sharing his thoughts with me and concluded our conversation.

Ironically, as if answering Frazier's prayers, volunteers at the shelter began taking Frazier and a few of the other dogs to one of the local dog parks a couple of times a week to run, which made all of them very happy.

I am pleased to report that one of the shelter volunteers adopted Frazier, finally giving him a forever home.

If you take your dog for a walk on a street frequented by cars, protect it from the possibility of running out into the traffic by walking it on a leash.

SYLVESTER

That Curious Cat

Sylvester is a beautiful gray male cat who is always very friendly and happy to see people. The ruler of the roost, Sylvester feels his job is to monitor all that is going on inside and outside the house. He is never afraid to tell what's going on with him, to report what's happening around him, or to answer any questions.

I've had the pleasure of visiting and communicating with Sylvester on several occasions. I always start by asking the animal that I am going to communicate with if I can speak with him or her. However, there is never a need to ask Sylvester. He usually starts the conversation by telling me what is happening. Once when I arrived, Sylvester ran up to me and greeted me with his usual "meow," and then rubbed against my hands and legs, purring. I asked him how he was, and he said, "I'm glad Mom's home." Sylvester's human companion had been out of town attending a seminar.

On another occasion, Sylvester's human companion asked me to question him about the whereabouts of one of her other cats, Precious, who I'll talk about in the next chapter. Sylvester said, "That cat? Left." I asked if he knew where she went or when she would be back, and he said, "Don't know." Sylvester always seems to know what's going on, but I'm not entirely sure he cares unless it involves him.

On another visit, I was asked to communicate with Bitsy (also a later story), a Pekingese mix that was found wandering the neighborhood. Sylvester was right there checking out what was going on. We decided to take Bitsy outside to potty before taking her to be bathed at the groomer. After Bitsy did her business and snooped around a little, we walked her to the garage where the car was parked. This was not the normal path around to the front drive, since walking around the other side was a shorter route and the one normally taken.

As we walked, Sylvester followed closely and asked, "Hey, where you going? What you doing?" I let Sylvester know that his mom was taking Bitsy to the groomer, and that she would be back soon. "So, stay here and be a good boy," I told him. Sylvester is always curious.

PRECIOUS

Pretty Little Precious

Precious is a beautiful black-and-white female cat that belongs to my friend. She is an indoor/outdoor cat, but spends most of the time outdoors. Often she will wander off for a day or two, exploring the area close to her home. On one particular occasion, Precious had disappeared while her human companion, my friend, was away at a seminar. My friend decided to wait a while for Precious to return since the cat's wandering ways were not uncommon. However, after a few days, Precious had still not returned.

I was asked if I could help find Precious or try to open a conversation with her to see where she was and if she was okay. I agreed to help, but I gently warned that the longer an animal is away, the harder it is to communicate with it. Often animals become busy with other things happening around them. It is also very draining on the communicator to try to sort out what has happened and maintain a long conversation with the lost animal once it has been gone for several days.

I established a connection with Precious by trying to draw her into my inner vision and to see if I could speak with her. As we entered the large subdivision community (more than five hundred homes), I began to see images of places Precious had been. Precious showed me the areas around a large lake. She also showed me a large screened-in back porch that was made of wood and stained white. The screen on the porch was black, and the porch covered most of the back of a tan-colored stucco house. The porch overlooked the lake and had a small, slightly wooded backyard.

Shortly before arriving at my friend's home, I asked Precious how she was, and she said, "I'm fine." I asked her what she was currently doing, and she said, "Exploring." She showed me more images of the many areas around the lake that she had visited. She said, "I've always wanted to explore these areas but never have . . . so, now I am."

I then asked her when she was coming home and told her that her mom missed her. She said she would come home, "When ready," which basically meant she would be back when she was good and ready. Unfortunately for the human companions of cats, good and ready could be in a few moments or a few weeks, if ever. I asked her why she had left, and she said, "Too many cats." Apparently, Precious needed her space from the other cats that resided at the house on a permanent and foster basis, and she decided that it was the right time for her to explore those areas that she had previously only viewed from a distance.

Once we arrived at the house where Precious lived, my wife, me, and our friend decided to walk around the neighborhood, around the lake, and through the brush on the lake's shore. At that time, I lost my connection with Precious. I was no longer able to speak with her and was no longer receiving images from her. After walking around the area, we asked neighbors if they had seen her. Unfortunately, no one had. After about an hour, we stopped at a bridge overlooking the lake for a rest. There, we decided that we should expand our search by driving around the neighborhood.

We drove all over the community looking for Precious. I continued to look for the home with the screened-in porch that she had shown me. I also made several attempts to reconnect with her. Shortly after driving over the bridge where we had paused to rest, I saw a site that had appeared to me in an earlier image. I immediately yelled, "Stop the car." My wife stopped the car and backed up slightly, so I could see between two houses, through the backyards, and across the lake, where I saw a white, wooden screened-in porch with a black-screened door on the backside of a tan-colored stucco house. The house had a small, slightly wooded backyard that overlooked the lake. I had not noticed this screened-in porch or house before, but it was identical to the image that Precious had shared with me nearly two hours before.

I was confident we would find Precious there, so we quickly drove to the house. On the way, Precious reappeared to me in a vision. She showed me that it indeed was the house where she had been. She showed me the backyard, trees, and lake. Wouldn't it be an awesome sight to arrive at the house, rush to the backyard, and find Precious waiting for us? Our hearts were pounding with excitement when we arrived at the house. We jumped out of the car and rushed to the backyard. Precious was not there. It was a major disappointment to all of us and left us feeling sad.

At times like this, some animal communicators would begin to question their abilities. However, I know that my gift is true. I have been able to help many animals and their human companions in the past. I know that the images I received and the words I heard from Precious were accurate. It's just that she had moved on from that area by the time we had arrived. After all, her original intent was to leave her home to explore, and that was exactly what she was doing.

Since that time, I have had a couple of conversations with Precious. She has shown me that she is still fine and being fed by a lady in the area. She still has her pretty pink collar on, but her identification tags have been lost. I believe by now Precious has moved on to her next mission. She has left our conversations behind, but I will never forget or give up on her, because I never know when she will want to speak with me, show me something, or come scampering back home. I will hold her and all the lost animals I may encounter in the future in my heart and surround them with protection and the highest good.

When searching for a lost animal (cat or dog, specifically), don't drive around yelling their name out of the car window. If they happen to hear you, you would be gone by the time they got to where you were. Instead, either yell for them from the front yard or backyard of your home or, if you do look for them by car, look silently.

ALISON

Pain in My Foot

A lison, a feral cat, took up residence at a friend's house. She seemed comfortable hanging around with the other cats on the back deck. However, she never took to people and will probably never fully trust humans. To this day, Alison will run into the bushes and brush that surround the house as soon as someone approaches her or the area she hangs around. She'll wait patiently, peeking her head out until she knows the coast is clear.

Not too long ago Alison seemed to have a hurt right leg, but my friend could never get close enough to her to check it out. One time while I was visiting, I managed to strike up a brief conversation with Alison. I asked if her leg was hurt. She glanced at me as if I was stupid and said, "Not leg . . . foot," and then she ran off. Animals are just like humans— some love to talk a lot and others can't wait for you to quit bugging them.

The next month, from out of nowhere, an alley cat appeared on the back porch of my friend's house and began to cause a lot of trouble with the other cats my friend was caring for. There are plenty of places at my friend's house to sleep and get out of the weather, and she sets out numerous dishes filled with cat food. However, the alley cat wanted it all! He wanted to take over. My friend tried to convince him to share, with no luck. The cat was not going to reason with anyone. My friend thought the only way to handle the situation was to scare the alley cat off by spraying water in his direction with a hose. Unfortunately, this also scared away

Alison. My friend assumed Alison would wait until the coast was clear and come back, but this time she did not return.

My friend asked me to try to have a conversation with Alison and let her know that it was okay to come home. I gave it my best attempt, but many days had gone by without a word, which was not a surprise since Alison had never been a big talker. Finally I managed to break through, and I asked her to come home. Alison said, "Feelings hurt." I told Alison that no one was mad at her and no one meant to offend her. I received a vision of her flipping her head away in disgust and walking away without another word. I suggested my friend put some wet food out on the lower level of the deck, and I would try to share the vision with Alison and let her know that the bowl of wet food was for her. My friend set the food out, and I was successful in showing Alison the vision of the food. But she did not return.

I still try to break through to find Alison and try to communicate with her. A lot of time has passed, and I can't seem to find her presence. I don't feel anything bad has happened to her, but I still pray that she is just being stubborn. As always, I continue to hope that she will return home one day.

Post a notice for rescue personnel on the windows by each door of your home. On each notice, include the number and type of animals that reside in your home as well as the name and phone number of your veterinarian. This will alert the rescue personnel that there are animals in the home and who has medical records for each pet on file in case there is a fire or other major catastrophe involving your home. Some rescue organizations like the Humane Society of the United States and the American Society for the Prevention of Cruelty to Animals (best known simply as the ASPCA) have this type of sticker for your window and may provide them upon request. Contact them for more information.

PENNY

One Shiny Penny

My wife and I volunteered at an adoption-day event at one of the local pet stores one Saturday. Our group had several adult cats and a litter of kittens on display for adoption. Though we weren't located in the front of the store, we appreciated being indoors away from the heat.

Five or six other no-kill rescue shelters were also there trying to find forever homes for their animals. One group gave their dogs a break from the heat by walking each of the dogs on a leash through the store. We were fortunate when one of the volunteers brought over a beautiful Pomeranian to visit with us. Her name was Penny, and she was a rusty-red color like a shiny new penny. She immediately brought a smile to my face and my wife's. We had been the parents of a beautiful red Pomeranian named Neecie. We had raised Neecie from a puppy while we were in college and had her through our early years of marriage. After fifteen blessed years, Neecie transitioned. We still miss her.

Penny was very open, calm, and eager to have a conversation with me. I began by asking her how she was. She said, "I'm fine," but she didn't seem overly confident in her words. She was a little timid but very sweet and kind. I'm sure she was still confused as to why she was there and not with her original owner. She seemed in good health, though some fur was worn thin on her back hindquarters. I asked her where she had come from and how she had ended up at the shelter. She began to show me the vision of an elderly woman. She showed me that the elderly woman was no longer able to take care of her and then she told me, "Too much." I told her that I was sorry, but explained that she was going to find another good home very soon and that she was very beautiful. I also explained to her that what had happened was not her fault and that she would be fine. She quietly accepted this and began wagging her tail as we petted her.

Toward the end of our visit, Penny rolled over on her back for a belly rub. We were happy to oblige this kind gesture. As I reached down to rub her belly, I realized she had recently had a litter of pups. I got the feeling the pregnancy had been unexpected and perhaps was too overwhelming for the elderly lady who had previously taken care of Penny. It's very sad that Penny has to go through the stress and doubt that comes with not having a permanent home. However, she is staying at a good no-kill shelter where she will be taken care of her until she finds her new home with a loving family.

SAYLOR

Set Out to Sea

Saylor is a small hound mix that has been a resident at the local shelter for quite some time. He was dropped off at the shelter by a couple that was going through a divorce, and neither of them wanted to keep him. Unfortunately, the couple did not explain to him what was happening and why he could no longer live with them. They simply dropped him off and left. From the time he entered the shelter, Saylor was withdrawn and aggressive toward everyone.

The only people who could get close to him were the volunteers and staff who were at the shelter on a daily basis.

Some of the staff asked me to have a conversation with Saylor, so I asked him if I could speak with him. He was open to a conversation, though quite agitated. Saylor began by saying, "No one likes me." He repeated this statement several times. He showed me how his human companions had dropped him off and left him alone at this strange place. He also showed me his dog run, which was located at the furthest end of the dog building. I tried to reassure him that everyone at the shelter *did* like him. I asked him if it would help if we moved him to one of the center runs where he could see everyone and be more involved, and he said, "I guess so." I also asked him if it would help if the staff spent more time with him, and he said, "Yes."

The staff at the shelter started paying more attention to Saylor, moved him to a center dog run, and even started letting him into the office when only a few people were around and it was quiet. Saylor seemed to enjoy the extra attention. Since we made the changes he has shown significant improvement. The staff has even gotten more comfortable around him. Though there is still a lot of healing to do, with time and a lot of love, I'm confident he will come around.

I have visited Saylor on a few occasions since then. Though he always puts up a defiant front, he is becoming less aggressive. He has made friends with a few of the dogs and enjoys being outside playing with them. Each time I see him, he runs toward the fence, barking. However, once he reaches the fence, he calms down and is willing to allow me to be in his presence.

I always stress that we should never give up on any animal. Consider the pain, fear, and uncertainty that Saylor went through, and then imagine how you would react under similar circumstances. With patience, attention, and love, Saylor will come around. He will just need a little more time to find his new forever home.

PEPE

It's Praying Time

On an extremely hot summer day, I walked out of our house into our screened-in porch. Often I would go out on the porch to look out over our backyard and beautiful southern garden. I often noticed that various types of bugs would hang out on the screens surrounding the porch. Day or night, you could usually find an assortment of spiders, flies, and other insects. Perhaps they stayed there to catch their dinner, take a rest, and get out of the elements.

On this particular day, I was graced with the presence of a praying mantis. To me, it is always exciting to see one of these majestic creatures. They are usually difficult to find away from plants—and more rare to find sunbathing on the screen of a porch.

I excitedly asked my wife to join me on the porch and take a look at our guest. She suggested I strike up a conversation with him. I had never tried to converse with an insect before and wasn't sure where a conversation with an insect would go. However, I decided to give it a try to see what would happen.

To my amazement, the conversation flowed freely. I started off by asking if I could speak with him. He said, in a superior tone, "Fine." I asked how he was, and he said, "Hot." I said, "But you like the heat," and he confirmed, "Yes." I asked him if he had a name and he said, "No." I asked him if he would like a name. With an apathetic tone, he said, "Sure." I suggested "Fred," the first name to come to mind. He defiantly said, "No!" I said, "How about Pepe?" Sarcastically, he said, "Fine."

I showed him that we had a lot of big plants within our screened-in porch and asked him if he would like to come inside where he would have more protection. He said, "No. Outside is better." I asked if there was anything he would like to tell me, and he did not respond. I suggested he walk over to the door later if he changed his mind about coming into the screened-in porch, and I would then let him in. Again, there was no response. I thanked him for the conversation and visit and told him that he was very handsome. He said, "Okay." As I walked away, I'm sure I heard him say, "Silly human."

If you are open and willing, you can communicate with anyone or any living thing. You just have to open your mind and your heart, then listen and let it flow. It's sort of like prayer, isn't it?

BLUE, DIXIE

Listening to the Blues in Dixie

One Saturday my wife and I volunteered at a cat-adoption event held at the local pet store. Our friend had several cats she had rescued from a feral cat colony. The cats had grown quite a bit since she rescued them as kittens. We met at my friend's house to pick up a table, some display items, and two cats—Blue and Dixie—to take to the event.

Both sweet, loving, beautiful Russian Blues, Blue is very quiet, while Dixie will talk your ear off. We put both into a carrier and placed them in the backseat for the twenty-minute ride to the pet store. Once we started the car, the fun began. While Blue sat quietly in her crate, Dixie began to talk . . . and talk . . . and talk. For the duration of the trip, she was like a young child wanting to know what was going on. She repeatedly said, "Doing, doing, doing?" I explained to her that we were going to the pet store to find her and Blue a new forever home. She understood what I had told her but the relentless "Doing, doing, doing?" continued. The only time Dixie changed her tune was when we stopped at a traffic light. Then there was a whole new phrase: "Now, now, now?" As in, "Are we there now?" or better known in the world of children, "Are we there yet?" I almost felt like saying, "Don't make me stop this car!"

Before bringing an animal into your home, do your research. Find out about the animal's exercise needs, how long it can be expected to live, whether it gets along well with children, whether it gets along well with other types of animals, how much time during the day you have to devote to the animal in the way of attention, how much it can cost to take care of the animal on an annual basis, etc. This will lead to a better choice of pets and less frustration on your part if you know what to expect before bringing a pet home.

HERSHEY

Sweet Like Chocolate

When I met Hershey, a beautiful Catalan Sheepdog, he had been suffering for some time from a degenerative disc located in his lower spine. Apparently this is a fairly common ailment for this breed of dog. The degenerative disc affected his ability to walk, stand, and move about. Hershey would have to undergo surgery to repair the disc and hopefully get his mobility back. It was a risky surgery, and there was the chance that it wouldn't solve his problem.

Hershey came through the surgery well, but then he faced a long recovery period. He had to attend rehabilitation therapy on a regular basis, and he struggled through the post-surgery pain. I had a chance to speak to Hershey a couple of times after his surgery. During our first conversation, I noticed a dark shadow surrounding him. It wasn't clear to me whether the dark shadow represented the pain Hershey felt or if it was the lingering anesthesia. I asked him how he felt, and he said, "Much better," and then said, "Still there." I was puzzled by his response and asked him to clarify. He then showed me his right back hip and hindquarter area. He obviously still felt some pain in the area.

When I asked him how the surgery went, he didn't show me any of the details from the experience, so I assumed the anesthesia had blocked the experience from his memory. However, he did show me the cage he was resting in after the surgery, and then showed me a tan and brown blanket. I finished our conversation by asking Hershey if he had anything he wanted me to tell his mom and dad and he said, "I show you. I show you," in a very determined tone. I realized that Hershey was emphatically stating that he would show everyone that he would fully recover and get back to his old self, healthy and strong. I told him that he would be fine, to feel better, and to work hard at his therapy. Hershey replied again, "I show you!"

The next day I had another brief chat with Hershey to see how he was doing. He stated again, "Much better." I noticed that the dark shadow that had surrounded him had been replaced by a bright, positive energy. Later that evening, I contacted Hershey's mom and dad to report the conversation I had had with him. When I mentioned to them that Hershey had repeatedly said to me, "I show you. I show you," Hershey's dad said he had asked Hershey while visiting him at the veterinarian's office to show him that he would be able to walk once he recovered. They confirmed that he was doing much better; in fact, they had brought him home from the veterinarian's office that afternoon. I'm sure the bright positive energy had been a combination of

Hershey feeling better and knowing that he would soon be going home.

Hershey continues to work hard at his therapy and is showing progress toward full recovery. I have no doubt that he will show us all!

Animal behavioral problems can be health related. If an animal's behavior changes suddenly and for no apparent reason, (e.g., your cat begins urinating outside of the litter pan) consult your veterinarian.

GRANDÉ

Is It Itsy-Bitsy

or Grandé?

A friend contacted my wife and me one Saturday to tell us she had found a lost older dog. She had seen the dog sitting out in the rain the day before, but assumed the dog belonged to one of the neighbors. When she saw the dog sitting in the same spot the next day, she worried that the dog was lost. She asked if I could try to speak with the dog to find out where it had come from. Our friend is a "cat person" and knows pretty much everything there is to know about cats. However, when it comes to dogs, she admits she is out of her element.

The dog was a cute, calm Pekingese mix that we thought was about twelve to fourteen years old (later we found out she was sixteen years old). She was a little hard of hearing, and her eyes were cloudy from cataracts, but she was very friendly and sweet. She even got along well with Mellow and Shady, two formerly feral cats our friend was fostering. We fed her, and she ate quickly, keeping Shady at bay away from her food.

We noticed that she had two collars around her neck. One was an electronic containment collar. The other was an old pink collar that had a Michigan rabies tag dated 2003. We found this odd since we live in Georgia, and at that time the tag was four years old. We contacted the veterinarian clinic in Michigan that was listed on the tag, but unfortunately, they had no records or address for the lost dog. They suggested we contact the county office in Michigan where the clinic was located. Since it was the weekend and that county office was closed until

Monday, we contacted the homeowners' association president of our friend's neighborhood. He posted the dog's information on the neighborhood's Web site in case someone was looking for her.

In the meantime, I tried to begin a conversation with the dog. Once she finished investigating the area where she was being kept and ate the amount of food she wanted, I was able to get her attention. I asked her what her name was and very quickly she said, "Bitsy." To make sure I heard her correctly, I asked again and she quickly replied, "Bitsy." I asked her where she came from and she said, "Moved." I had assumed that she must have meant the move from Michigan to Georgia. I tried to get more clarification about where she had moved to, but she quickly lost interest in our conversation. I did the best I could, but we really didn't know much more than when we had first met the dog.

Later that night, our friend contacted us to let us know that someone in the neighborhood had checked the Web site and had called to claim the dog. Our friend returned Bitsy to her owner, who lived very near where Bitsy had been found. As our friend let Bitsy out of the car onto the driveway, she heard the electronic containment collar beep. The collar worked properly, but the dog still walked through the containment area and ignored the "slight correction" that the collar gave. I've seen high-energy dogs ignore the correction, but never a sixteen-year-old Pekingese.

When our friend gave Bitsy to the gentleman, he confirmed that she did live there but that her name was Grandé. When I heard this, I wondered who the heck Bitsy was. Could it have been a nickname? Was there another animal in the house, or was this a name that she would rather be called? Face it, Grandé is not a very suitable name for a small Pekingese—at least that's my opinion, and I'm sticking to it.

I was very puzzled about my conversation with Bitsy . . . oops! I mean Grandé. How could I have been so far off? I know what she told me during our conversation. Grandé's owner told our friend that the dog was incontinent and often wandered off. It was a little scary to think about such a fragile, elderly little dog wandering around on her own. Maybe she was confused in what she was telling me . . . or maybe I was confused. Let's just say that communicating with an animal is not an exact science—the animal usually says whatever is on its mind when you ask it a question. I guess I was just a little bit(sy) off on this one.

LILLY

Isn't She Great?

One Labor Day weekend we visited our cousins at their horse farm in Huntsville, Alabama. Their farm consists of a little more than ten acres of open pasture and cleared wooded areas. It's always nice to visit the farm to see their four horses, a few house cats, and their dogs: Buster and Tank. On this day we got to see their newest guest, a beautiful Great Pyrenees they named Lilly, who had appeared at the farm a few weeks earlier. They were not sure where she had come from or whom she had belonged to. She wore a blue, tattered collar, but they couldn't get close enough to see if there were any tags because Lilly was very timid and wouldn't let anyone near her. Our cousin's husband could get close enough to set out food, but no one else could approach her without her quickly running off.

Lilly would approach Buster and Tank, but she was not comfortable enough to stay and play with them. She did feel comfortable around the horses. This is fairly typical of a Great Pyrenees. They are wonderful dogs to have around the farm, preferring to stay in the open fields around horses or cattle. They are known to guard livestock by chasing off any predators that may be in the area.

I thought I would try to get close enough to Lilly to ask how she was and to get her attention long enough to have a conversation. At first, Lilly didn't want any part of me or to listen to anything I had to say. Each time I approached her, she would run away just far enough so that she could keep an eye on me. I did get close enough to be able to tell that she had been on her own for a while. She was small in size for a Great Pyrenees, with dirty, matted fur. Not only was she scared, but I also kept picking up that she had been abused and chased off from her last home.

I decided to go to Plan B, resorting to treats to help coax Lilly out. I had brought with me some high-quality treats to give to all the dogs. Buster and Tank were more interested in running and playing ball than partaking in the treats. However, Lilly was more than accepting. Though she still would not let me feed the treats to her by hand, she would get within five feet of me. As I tossed the treats to her, she would pick them up, look at me, and quickly eat them. We went through this process for a little while, and it seemed to establish a bond of trust between us.

I took advantage of the situation to open a conversation channel with her. Though she wasn't interested in replying to my words, she listened. I assured her that everything was okay and that we were not going to hurt her. I told her that we would like to get close enough to her to see if she was healthy, needed any medical attention, and to clean her up a little. We were not going to rush her, and she could come over to us on her terms. Lilly seemed to accept what I said and calmed down.

I left the farm that day feeling very good about my chat with Lilly. I felt that, given some time and patience, she would come around. However, what happened later that day was a little unexpected. We received a call the day after we left the farm to let us know that Lilly had been approached by our cousin's husband, and Lilly allowed him to pet her. He even managed to give her a bath and check her for injuries. Fortunately, Lilly looked fine and responded well to the attention. A few days later, they took Lilly to the groomer. She did well at the groomer and looked beautiful.

Our cousins sent an e-mail to their friends to see if they could find Lilly a good forever home. Eventually someone stepped forward and expressed interest in adopting Lilly. The lady was from Tennessee and ran a Great Pyrenees rescue sanctuary.

She came down the next weekend to visit with Lilly, and there was an immediate connection between them. A couple of weeks later, Lilly was off to her new home.

CUPID, TAWNY

You Can't Hold Tawny Back

If you recall, I spoke about Tawny in a previous tale. Tawny is a beautiful tabby that lost one of her eyes to an eye infection. Tawny and her best friend and brother, Cupid, were inseparable. They had been together since birth and had spent more than two years at the shelter together.

One day, an elderly lady and her son came to the shelter looking for a companion that would keep the son company but not need a lot of attention. He lived in a cozy apartment in his mother's basement that had a big picture window overlooking the fields of their farm. It seemed like an ideal location for a cat or two.

After spending some time with the cats, he became attached to Tawny. He felt that he could provide her with the attention and forever home she deserved. We tried to convince him that Tawny and Cupid were a pair and that he would have greater success if he adopted both. However, his mother was not convinced. She really didn't like the idea of one cat, let alone two. After a lot of discussion, and following a home visit, the adoption team decided to take a chance and let Tawny go home with the mother and son without Cupid. This became one of those times when the team should have followed their instincts.

Tawny tried to adapt to her new environment. However, she never became comfortable in her new home; the man did not show the patience needed to gain her trust, and, as I said, the mother had never wanted the cat in the first place. The match was doomed from the beginning.

After a few days, the man returned to the shelter. He and his mother had gotten into an argument, and he thought it would be best to return Tawny. He had placed Tawny in a small cat carrier that was sitting in his backseat, but he had not latched the gate to the carrier completely. As he struggled to close the gate, Tawny jumped out and ran under a parked truck in the shelter's lot. Everyone at the shelter scrambled to reach Tawny from under the truck, but she made a run for it. She ran around the corner of the building and headed toward the back of the shelter. By the time they got there, she was gone.

Behind the shelter stands a dog building, several fenced dog runs, and a few storage sheds. Behind the dog runs are dense, thorny woods. Several wide-open fields that belong to the neighbors of the shelter surround this area. In other words, there are plenty of places for a cat to hide or get lost.

The volunteers and staff at the shelter searched the area for Tawny. They looked under the storage sheds, around the dog runs, in the woods, in the fields, and around the shelter. Tawny was nowhere to be found.

The pursuit went on into the next day. After continuously running into dead ends, they decided to contact me to see if I could help—almost two full days after Tawny had disappeared. As I've mentioned, the more time that passes, the more difficult it becomes to make contact. This is especially true with cats. Their survival mode starts to kick in, and they focus on other things instead of returning home. This was especially true for Tawny, who had seen numerous homes in her lifetime.

Tawny and I did share a special bond. I had come to visit her at the shelter on many occasions, and she had always been receptive to me. She would jump down from the shelf where her cat bed was perched, rub against me several times, purr, and then jump in my lap for some dedicated attention. I always felt that she was a special girl and admired her for her tenacity. When considering all that she had been through, I thought she was truly amazing.

I began to focus on making contact with Tawny in hopes of learning more about where she was. Surprisingly, we connected quickly and easily. She was definitely scared, and she wasn't certain where she was. She began to show me a field where she had to "high-step" when she walked in order to see above the grass. I asked her if she could see the gray building, which was the shelter. She said, "I've never seen that building." This was puzzling to me at first, since she had spent a large portion of her life there. However, I realized that she had never been outside of the shelter and had no idea what it looked like from the outside.

I asked Tawny if she could go back to where she had jumped out of the cat carrier. If she could make it back there, she could wait on the steps and someone would come get her and take her back inside to be with Cupid again. But Tawny was scared and unsure of where to go. The connection that I had with Tawny during this conversation was very strong. She showed me the area where she was walking, and I saw her approach a metal fence with horizontal wiring connected to wooden posts. The fence design was typical of the area. As Tawny approached the fence, something terrible happened. The picture she was showing me went blank, and I was suddenly surrounded by a bright white light. I felt a sharp pain in my chest that lingered for about five minutes. I had never experienced anything like it before. I feared the worst, and tried desperately to reconnect with Tawny. This was not to be; I had lost track of her.

I immediately jumped into my car and drove to the shelter. During the drive, I tried to reestablish my connection with Tawny, without success. I hoped and prayed that she had not transitioned during our conversation. When I arrived at the shelter, I joined the others in the search for her. We drove around to see if I could identify the area that Tawny had shown me. However, I could not locate the exact spot since the image she showed me with the fencing surrounding an ankle-deep, grassy field was not unique to the area.

The volunteers asked me over and over if she had transitioned and, if so, could I help them locate the body. I was reluctant at first to give my opinion because of the unfamiliar, simultaneous events that I had experienced. Plus, I had asked Cupid if he had heard from Tawny while I was experiencing all of this, and he said, "Yes, she's gone." Because of what had happened during my experience with Tawny, combined with what Cupid had said, I concluded that she had probably transitioned.

The volunteers asked if I could continue to try to connect with Tawny just in case she was still alive. Or, if she had transitioned, maybe she could tell us whether she was now okay, what had happened to her, and where her remains were located. I told them I would continue to try to communicate with her. However, if she was in the transition process, it may take a while to connect. I explained that when an animal transitions, it goes through a regeneration process that restores its source energy. This process could take days, weeks, or months.

The volunteers also asked if they should set out humane traps around the shelter just in case she returned. Honestly, I did not hold much hope in this, but I saw no harm in trying.

Since I was having no luck reaching Tawny, I thought it would be a good idea to see if her brother could shed any light on the matter. Cupid had stayed in contact with Tawny throughout this ordeal. He stayed close to the window to keep an eye out for her, leaving only when we had set a cat crate outside of his room. Once we removed the crate from the area, he went back to the window. I asked him if he knew where Tawny was and what had happened. He said that he had to "Be here for Tawny" and "She's gone."

For four weeks I continued my efforts to reconnect with Tawny. Volunteers asked me daily if I had had any luck. When I could not reestablish a communication connection with her after this length of time, I began to wonder if I would ever have an opportunity to speak with her again.

One day early in the fifth week since her disappearance, Tawny finally came to me while I was meditating. I asked her if she was well. She told me, "I am well. I'm feeling fine." I told her that we missed her. She said, "Miss you." I asked her if there was anything I could tell Cupid. She said, "He knows . . . I told him . . . I'm fine . . . much better." I asked, "Are you okay?" She said, "I'm fine . . . don't worry . . . no more worry." I asked if there was anything else she wanted to say. She said, "No . . . I'm fine." I told her that she would always be with us and if she needed me or wanted to talk, to let me know. She said, "Okay," and then the connection ended.

During this conversation, Tawny appeared to be healthy and whole. She even wanted to make sure I knew it was she by showing me the area where her eye had been removed. It was still unclear as to where she was or if she had transitioned. However, I assumed that since so much time had passed and she was now trying to reassure us that she was fine, she had transitioned. I was still not receiving a strong "in-body" feeling from her, though I assumed she was doing well. But you know what they say about assuming. And boy, did I find out I was wrong.

Six weeks had passed since Tawny had gone missing, and I had had only one brief conversation with her. Was it even possible that she was still in-body? Could she have survived such an ordeal as losing her eye and then being on her own for six weeks? She had never been in the wild; was it even possible that she could still be alive?

Then one morning a volunteer had checked a humane trap that he had set near one of the storage sheds. Usually, only raccoons or opossums were caught in one of these traps. But on this day, it was a cat, and not just any cat. It was Tawny! It seemed too good to be true. She was severally dehydrated, hungry, and dirty, but she was alive.

Tawny was taken to the local veterinarian to be examined and given fluids. The veterinarian noticed that one of her feet was injured. After having the foot X-rayed, it was evident that something had run over her foot and crushed it. It could not be repaired, but she seemed to manage with the injury just fine. We were all excited that she was back with us, and she seemed thrilled to be back as well. Cupid also appeared to be more at peace, his spirits renewed.

Though I was extremely happy about Tawny's return, I was also confused. How could what I had experienced (severe chest pain and white light), coupled with what Cupid had told me, been anything other than Tawny transitioning? After several conversations with other practitioners in my field, I gained a better understanding of what had really happened. The sharp pain coincided with Tawny having her foot crushed. When an animal—especially cats—are lost and have suffered a traumatic event, they tend to go into a protective state where their physical bodies all but completely shut down. This allows them to protect and heal themselves. Tawny had experienced this and spent the six weeks allowing her foot to heal. She was able to briefly speak to me after five weeks in order to tell me that she was well and everything would be fine.

I learned two very valuable lessons from this experience:

1. Never assume or read into a communication you are having with an animal. Let them tell you exactly what is going on.

2. Never rule out a "wonder cat" named Tawny.

Tawny got to take a short trip to a volunteer's beach house for the winter. I am pleased to say that she is now healthy and living in her new forever home. After a while her foot healed, though it is now a bit crooked. She gets along quite well and interacts with the other cats in the home.

Keep the information on the identification tags that your pet wears up-to-date. If your pet gets loose, the tags will be the first thing people look for to help locate its owners. Make sure your pet's name, your address, and your phone number are included on the identification tags.

SCARLET

Where Could
Scarlet Be?

When one of our friends decided to replace her flooring and paint some of the rooms in her house, she had to move most of the furniture in the house to other rooms or into the garage. Not an overnight fix, the project caused quite a stir in the household, especially among her cats.

One evening as my friend prepared the cats' evening meals, she realized that all of the cats had shown up except one, Scarlet, which was highly unusual. While the other cats ate, my friend looked in all of Scarlet's usual hiding places and then checked each room in the three-story house. Scarlet was nowhere to be found, and my friend began to worry that she had left a door open while moving the furniture and Scarlet had ventured outdoors. My friend asked if I could connect with Scarlet and find out where she was.

The connection I made with Scarlet was strong, and she was open to conversing with me. She showed me that she was still in the house. She then showed me a door that had been left open that was usually closed, and she communicated that she had taken the opportunity to investigate the area. Unfortunately, that was all the information Scarlet was willing to share, and it was still unclear to me exactly where she was hiding.

My friend, puzzled as to where Scarlet might be, contacted another one of our friends and told her what Scarlet had told me. They put their heads together and determined that the door leading out to the garage had been left open. Some of the furniture had been moved into the garage, so they decided Scarlet was probably hiding beneath one of the chairs or couch. Sure enough, she had crawled up under the lining of the couch and was hiding out. She didn't seem to care if anyone found her or her new hiding place.

MISCHIEF, ANGEL

Mischief Is No Angel

My friend has two cats: Mischief, who is fourteen years old, and Angel, who is thirteen years old. About two years ago, Angel started urinating in various areas of my friend's house instead of using her litter pan. At first it was sporadic, but then it began happening consistently, and after six months, my friend asked me to have a conversation with Angel, and also talk to Mischief about a different issue while I was at it.

I called my friend, and we talked for a few minutes about things happening in our lives. During our conversation, I sensed that Angel was in the room and asked my friend if I could introduce myself since it is always appropriate to introduce yourself to an animal and ask for its permission to hold a conversation. This is true whether the conversation takes place in person or over the phone.

While I was asking Angel if we could speak, my friend saw Angel turn her head and move her ears as though she were listening to someone. Each time I asked a question of Angel she would react with another movement of her body. She happily spoke with me and told me what was going on in her life. Angel was concerned with all of the changes happening in her household. She kept repeating, "Changes, changes, changes." I asked my friend if she had recently changed something in the house or in her routine. There had been no changes, but Angel persisted with, "Changes, changes, changes."

As you know, animals dislike changes in their normal routine. The least little change in their routine throws them off. I asked my friend again about any possible changes and if she had changed her routine or was spending more time out of the house. Bingo! My friend had changed her work hours, and was coming home later than usual. Angel was upset because she didn't know what time my friend would be home. I instructed my friend to tell Angel the time she would be home each evening before she left for work. This would put Angel's mind at ease knowing when she would be home. I then told Angel that her mommy would be telling her where she was going when she left the house and what time she would be back. My friend started the next day telling Angel and Mischief where she was going and what time she would be home, and Angel stopped urinating on the furniture that very day. Angel now waits in the living room for the door to open at the time my friend is scheduled to arrive, whereas before she would be in other areas of the house and come out only when her name was called.

Though she had returned to urinating exclusively in her litter box, I continued to communicate with

Angel so that I could get to know her better. I found out that she normally keeps to herself and appears publicly only on her terms. However, she did seem to enjoy talking to me. I asked her what she thought of her pal Mischief. She said, halfheartedly, "She's okay." I asked if there was anything that she needed. She said, "Treats . . . more, more." Apparently she gets a special stinky treat at night, and of course, she wanted them more often. She then went on to show me her beautiful black tail. She kept repeating, "Beauty, beauty, beauty." This was to make sure that everyone knew she was beautiful and her tail was her best feature.

My friend then asked me why Angel would frequently let out loud noises, like she was howling. I asked Angel about the howling, and she replied, "It's not howling, I'm singing. I'm singing to Mommy, and she needs to sing along." To this day Angel and her mommy are still howling . . . I mean singing!

Anxious to get in on the conversation, Mischief spoke up. Mischief is a beautiful tuxedo cat that is always under her mommy's feet. I asked Mischief if we could speak, and she eagerly agreed. She promptly showed me her favorite toys, treats, and litter box. She explained to me that she shared each of these with Angel but would prefer to have her own. I asked her what she thought of Angel, and she said, "She's all right," and then whispered, "She's bossy." (Of course, this was said when Angel had temporarily left the room.) She went on to show me all of the wonderful plants that her mommy had around the house. She particularly liked the new plant with long and narrow leaves that mommy got for Christmas. She liked to rub her face on the leaves and chew on them. I later found out that my friend had received a spider plant as a Christmas present.

I suggested to my friend that she remove the plants from the floor and put them high on a counter away from the cats. Though the cats liked to chew on the plant leaves, it was probably not healthy.

As my conversation wound down with Mischief, I felt Angel come back into the room. All of a sudden, she began running around the room and then up the staircase to the top of the landing, where she stopped and began howling. My friend explained that Angel followed the same pattern and routine at least once a day. I asked Angel what the chasing was all about, and she said, "Chasing skinny black cat." She explained that the cat appears, and she chases her. She said, "It's a game." I asked my friend if she had a skinny black cat that I didn't know about. She said that she didn't. Angel then showed me the cat and said that she lived in the back garden area under the ground. She would appear in the house each night for Angel to play chase with. I asked my friend if she had buried a cat in the back garden. She said that she hadn't, but perhaps the previous owners had.

The next day my friend called the previous owners of her home and confirmed that they had buried their black cat in the backyard when it had died. This was the same area where my friend had planted her garden. Apparently, Angel and the ghost of the skinny black cat had become playmates.

Before buying a plant for your home, find out if the plant is poisonous to animals. The reactions to the toxic substance in some plants can range from mild nausea to death. I had a family member whose cat died because it ate part of a leaf from an Easter lily. Other common houseplants that are poisonous are philodendrons and poinsettias.

EFFIE, OLIVER

Call Me Pretty Boy

Effie, a long-haired, orange-and-white female cat, and her partner, Oliver, a shorthaired, sandy-colored male cat, were rescued strays that were taken in by a friend of mine from church. She wanted to make sure they were happy and that she was doing everything in the manner they liked.

I first struck up a conversation with Oliver, who was anxious to show me all of his wonderful toys and litter box. Animals are always proud of the things that belong only to them, and they are excited to share images of them with me. Oliver went on to show me his venison and fish food that he likes so well. He also told me he wanted some more stinky treats. (Now, where have I heard that before?)

My friend said that Oliver likes to lick himself constantly, especially around the belly, and she wondered why. I asked Oliver why he licked his belly and if it itched? He said, "I lick my fur to stay small. I want to stay small." Oliver was not a particularly hefty cat, but he thought he was. He felt that it was important to stay small. I told Oliver that he was fine the way he was, and he was a very pretty boy. He seemed to like that notion and really liked the idea that he was a pretty boy. He liked it so much that he told me that he no longer wanted to be called Oliver. Instead, he wanted to be called "Pretty Boy."

When I asked Effie if she were happy in the new house, she said, "Yes, happy . . . why not?" This confirmed that all was well with her. She liked to snoop in any new bags and boxes her human companion brought into the house. She also enjoyed listening to music while my friend was away, especially jazz. The only thing she didn't like was Oliver hogging the litter box. Effie went on to show me that she had some crusty substance around her nose, and she was very sensitive to smells. The aromatherapy and candles in the house definitely had a negative impact on her allergies. My friend agreed not to use them around Effie.

TESA

When Will They Ever Leave?

One of my friends has a nice quiet home, and she likes it this way. The home consists of my friend and her husband and three pets: a Pomeranian, a Pekingese, and a long-haired Calico cat named Tesa. Though you'd think that the animals' human companions would run the household, or at least the two dogs, this is not the case. Tesa is queen of her domain!

Tesa rules with her elegant style and loving ways. Everybody gets along very well with this arrangement. Tesa is not demanding; she just likes things to be the way she likes them. (Don't we all?) Everything was pure bliss for Tesa until the day their new houseguests arrived.

One of my friend's sons and his wife moved in for a week or so until their new home was finished being built. As these things seemingly always happen, weeks tend to turn into months. It was a challenge having two more people in the house and adjusting to all the new habits and energy that came with it. However, all of them managed to get along, except for the third visitor they brought with them—their black-and-white cat.

It became evident very quickly that "queen" Tesa was not to have any part of the intruder, who proved to be too much of a disturbance for her quiet domain. And no matter how hard she tried, Tesa could not control this new addition to the household.

Tesa began trying to reestablish her control by marking her territory. She felt that establishing what was hers would deter the unwanted guest from taking over. It was a futile attempt, as the new cat's exuberance and energy tested Tesa at every turn. Ultimately, Tesa retreated to the master bedroom and spent most of the day in hiding.

My friends asked me to chat with Tesa and try to convince her that this new arrangement was only temporary. Tesa was very open and honest with me. She could not handle the new energy in the household. She had been happy with the way things were before the new cat arrived, and she wanted things back to normal. Tesa told me that the other cat was "crazy," and she called the house "my place." She explained that she was marking the house to try to make it safe and to drive the other cat away. When this didn't work, she retreated and gave up hope.

I tried to comfort Tesa and told her that the new cat and people in the house would be gone in one month. I explained that she needed to stop marking the house, since it was causing stress for her momma and dad. I told her that her momma and dad would get another litter box and put it in the master bathroom, and they would put her food in the bathroom as well. This way she would not have to interface with the other cat. Tesa said that this "may be better"; she "didn't know" if it would work, but she would try.

The new arrangement helped, but it still wasn't perfect. Things would not be blissful until the house-guests left and all of the old routines were back in place. I think we can all understand how Tesa feels: been there, done that!

Animals like to have their own things. So, if circumstances permit, provide each animal within your household with its own food dish, litter pan, toys, bed, etc.

BLAIR, SAYLOR,
FRAZIER

Let's Go Outside for a While

Frazier and Saylor—whom you've read about in previous tales—and a third dog, Blair, had been brought to the local rescue shelter from homes that were in turmoil and full of drama. Plus, none of their human companions had explained to these dogs why they were brought to the shelter. Obviously, the dogs were scared and confused. They felt that they needed to protect themselves, and they retreated within themselves and would not let anyone near them—human or animal.

Over time, they grew to somewhat trust a few of the people who were at the shelter on a daily basis. However, they continued to show aggression toward most people and animals.

At the shelter, the dogs are usually divided up into playgroups for their time outside. The playgroups are determined by size, breed, and temperament of the dogs. The team at the shelter does a great job determining which dogs would play best together. But sometimes this can be a trial-by-error scenario. If a particular dog does not get along well with the others, then it is moved to another playgroup. The dog is moved until the team can find the best playgroup for it.

Frazier, Saylor, and Blair had a hard time finding a playgroup that they were comfortable in. They were all strong but fearful dogs. One day it was recommended that all three be put into the same playgroup. This proved to be the perfect solution, and the three dogs became the best of friends. This arrangement worked out so well that the shelter volunteers and employees wondered if they should keep the three together all the time. During playtime they were always kept together, but they were brought inside to their individual runs in the dog building at night. This created a lot of stress for each of these dogs. They did not like the energy and noise when they joined the other dogs in the building.

As a solution, a member of the team suggested letting Frazier, Saylor, and Blair use one of the shelter's infrequently used outdoor dog runs as a permanent sleeping area. They would be near each other yet apart from the other dogs, where it would be quieter. And they could be moved inside during inclement weather.

I was asked if I could have a conversation with each of the dogs and ask them if they were agreeable to being moved to the unused dog run. I started my first conversation with Frazier. Frazier told me that "Outside is okay, with others." He liked the other dogs and liked playing and running with them. Frazier told me that he wanted to be "like others" and not by himself, or sectioned off with just Saylor and Blair. This was not a good sign that Frazier would be receptive to the new plan.

I then spoke with Saylor, who concurred with Frazier by saying, "Outside okay, with others." He then said that he preferred "small, not big dogs." Saylor was fine with Frazier and really liked Blair. However, he was not too keen on being outside in a different place from the other dogs.

I finally spoke to Blair, and she said, "Outside, okay, with Saylor." She said that she and Saylor were "buddies," and she would be happy anywhere as long as Saylor was there.

It appeared that the grand plan was not going to be well received by the group. It would be fine to keep the three dogs together but not isolated from the rest of the dogs. As much as they hated being inside with all of the other dogs, it would be worse to be outside. All three wanted to be accepted by everybody—humans and dogs alike, but they just hadn't managed to figure out how.

Socialize puppies as early as possible. This includes exposing them to other animals as well as children and other adults.

BLACKIE

Blackie in the Woods

A friend of mine has a gray-and-black striped male cat named Blackie that she and her family took in when he was a kitten. They had found him half frozen from the winter cold and nursed him back to health in their home, where they had many other cats and dogs. He grew to be big and strong, though somewhat of a loner. It was not uncommon for Blackie to go off alone to explore in the woods surrounding the back portion of their property. It was also not uncommon for raccoons, opossums, squirrels, and other animals to search the backyard for food. On more than one occasion, coyotes were spotted in the woods, but they had never ventured into my friend's yard. That was about to change.

One day some neighbors heard what they thought was a pack of dogs. When they looked out their window to investigate, they saw what they thought were three large dogs chasing the cats around the yard, but they quickly realized that the dogs were actually coyotes. The cats ran in all different directions: into the garage, up onto the porch, up into the trees, and into the woods. All had escaped the scary ordeal and were safe. Blackie, being most comfortable with the woods, ran to hide there.

My friend thought Blackie would return once the coast was clear, but days went by and there was no sign of him. At that point she decided to contact me to see if I could communicate with him to ensure that he was okay and to let him know that it was safe for him to return home. Of course I agreed to help in any way that I could, but I reminded her that it is sometimes difficult to convince cats that have been frightened that it is safe to come home—especially after they have been chased away by coyotes.

I tried for three days to open a communication link with Blackie, but had little success. I could see Blackie and knew that he was in-body and fine physically. Each day that I connected with him I could see a white shadow or silhouette around him. I could also see the dense woods surrounding the back part of the yard and a creek running nearby. I knew Blackie was hiding in the woods. I could also see two sets of eyes staring back at me. One was Blackie's, the other set was dark, and I couldn't make out what animal they were coming from. Could it have been one of the coyotes waiting in the wings for Blackie to appear?

On the fourth day, I finally broke through and was able to communicate with Blackie. I asked him what had happened and all he could say was, "I was scared and I ran." I explained to him that it was safe to come home and that his mommy was waiting for him. Blackie said, "Scared and dark." It was clear that he wasn't ready to venture back home.

I asked Blackie where he was, and he showed me blue-gray lattice beneath the wooden porch. This is where he had been hiding and felt secure. I told Blackie that it was safe to come back home, and he should do so in a hurry. He said that "those dogs" would get him. I told him that the dogs were no longer there, and I would tell them to stay away from him and his home. He didn't seem to believe me and said he would return "later."

After repeated attempts, I have not been able to convince Blackie that it is safe enough for him to come home. My ability to communicate with him is still strong, though, and the white shadow or silhouette has been lifted. The good news is that Blackie has been spotted near a house that has blue-gray lattice beneath the wooden porch.

There is currently an ongoing debate about whether the microchips implanted as identification tags in animals can cause cancer. I am not a medical expert, but both of my dogs have microchips. I did this because collars with identification tags can fall off if a pet gets loose or runs away. The microchips can be scanned by veterinarians and animal control facilities and have proved useful countless times in reuniting pets with their owners.

PUMPKIN, MISSY, BEBE, BIGGY, & SCOOTER

Blackie's Running Mates

S everal cats and a dog lived with Blackie, the lost cat from the previous chapter. All of the cats were involved when the coyotes appeared, and the dog was well aware of what was happening. I took the opportunity to see what was going on with each of them, get their accounts of the attack, and see if they knew where Blackie was.

I first spoke with Scooter, the dog. Scooter is an older white poodle–fox terrier mix that stays indoors most of the time. Scooter seemed to have a lot of medical issues resulting from allergies. He showed me that his right eye had an allergic reaction to something, and his skin constantly itched. It was confirmed that he was on allergy medication for his skin issues. Scooter told me that the medication actually worsened his itching and skin condition. His allergies caused him great stress, and he had begun urinating indoors to show that he was not doing well on the medication. I suggested to his human companions that they contact Scooter's veterinarian to see if there was something else that could be done for him.

I asked Scooter if he had seen what had happened when the coyotes arrived. He said he had not because he was inside, but he had heard the commotion. He wondered why he couldn't be outside all the time to see what was going on. He said, "Outside, more better." I explained to him that the yard was not fenced, and his human companions feared he might wander away or that the coyotes could reappear. He seemed quite puzzled by this and promptly exclaimed, "The cats do." He figured that if the cats were allowed outside whenever they wanted, he should be able to go out as well. It was hard to disagree with his logic. I told him his job was to stay inside to protect and monitor what was going on there.

I then spoke with each of the cats. I started with the orange tabby named Pumpkin, who was difficult to pin down for a conversation because he was busy running around the house. I introduced myself and asked if I could have a conversation with him. He said, "Yes," and then said his name was Pumpkin and he was the "scamper cat." His job was to scamper around the house checking on everything and everybody. I confirmed with my friend, who laughed, and was amazed that he called himself "Scamper Cat." My friend once had a cat that was named Scamper Cat, but that was before Pumpkin came into her home. Obviously, Pumpkin had picked up on this and assumed the new role and title.

I reconnected with Pumpkin and asked him if he knew where Blackie was, and he said, "He's gone. He ran. I hid," telling me exactly what had happened when the coyotes had appeared. I asked if he had spoken to Blackie since Blackie had run off. Since Blackie wasn't physically there, Pumpkin seemed puzzled as to how he could talk to him. I explained to Pumpkin how he could have a conversation with Blackie even though Blackie was away. He agreed to try, but his efforts were unsuccessful. I then asked if there was anything else he would like to share with me. He promptly showed me a small, two-colored ball with a bell inside. I asked if it was his ball, and he said, "Yes. I like it." It was clear that Pumpkin was more concerned about his ball and scampering around than worrying about Blackie.

I then turned my attention to Bebe, a gray-and-black striped tabby. A very strong and proud cat with a rather matter-of-fact attitude, Bebe takes care of herself and feels that everyone around her should honor her. She was initially aloof and somewhat reluctant to talk to me. However, when I asked her about Blackie, her demeanor changed. She became anxious and somewhat afraid. She looked around and then exclaimed, "He ran. He ran. I stay." She said it was dogs [coyotes] outside who chased Blackie away, and then stated, "Dogs are bad. Not all dogs, just outside dogs." I asked Bebe if she was okay and if there was anything she needed. She resumed her strong, proud demeanor, and showed me that she wanted her own tan scratching post with smelly stuff [catnip] on it.

I opened a new conversation with Biggy, a brown-and-black male tabby with white boots. Although he first seemed quite bothered by the notion of speaking with me, Biggy reluctantly gave in. I asked him if he was okay, and he said, "I'm fine." I asked if he had anything to tell me, and he sternly said, "No, I'm fine." I asked if he knew where Blackie went and he said, "No, I ran the other way." He said he did not know where Blackie was and then he said, "Outside dogs are bad."

The last cat I spoke with was a small female brown tabby named Missy, who was not around when I first tried to talk to her. She went missing for an entire day, and my friend was worried sick. Fortunately, Missy reappeared at the house the next day. I asked her where she had been, and she said she had been looking for Blackie and she had only returned because it had started raining. She kept saying, "He's out there. He's out there." She wanted to look for Blackie again but thought she should stay close to home and away from the big outside dogs.

Although none of the conversations with Blackie's running mates yielded additional information that would lead to his whereabouts, they all seem to be moving on with their lives in his absence.

There is a difference between feral cats and stray cats. Stray cats have been separated from their families through abandonment or loss and are often wary of people. They often remain friendly and, if caught, can be adopted into a family again. Feral cats are usually the offspring of stray or feral cats and grow up without any human interaction. They survive in colonies with other stray and/or feral cats. Unless they are kittens under the age of five weeks old, feral cats typically cannot be tamed or brought into a home environment.

MAX

Pushed to the Max

A friend who had been fostering Max, a black lab mix, for the local shelter had grown quite attached to the dog and decided to adopt him.

A few months after he had become a part of the family, Max became mysteriously ill. He had stopped eating and had vomited on one occasion. My friend asked me to try to determine if his condition was serious enough that she needed to take him to the veterinarian. I reminded her that I am not a veterinarian and that she would have to be the one to make this decision. I agreed to speak with Max and scan his energy to try to determine what was going on, but I explained that no matter what Max told me, she may want to take him to the veterinarian as a precaution. She agreed she would decide what was best after I spoke with Max.

As soon as I opened my conversation with Max, I could tell he was nervous and anxious. I asked him what was wrong, and he said, "Changes, changes." I asked him what he meant, and he showed me all of the changes happening around him. There were two new foster dogs, a new house, a new baby, new baby gates, another young child running around, new food . . . His head was spinning! I described for my friend what Max had shown me and what he was experiencing. All of the things Max had shown me were true, and all of them had happened over the past couple of months. She empathized with Max; her head was spinning, too!

I explained that everyone would adjust in time, and I did not feel there were any real medical problems with Max. All of his issues were centered on the stress he felt due to all of the recent changes. I suggested that she and her family get settled first. Max was feeding off of their anxiety, and he probably would not calm down until they were at ease. I also suggested they comfort Max by telling him he was special, and letting him know that this was his forever home. His job was to protect his home and to keep an eye on the children.

Once everyone had settled into their new home and routine, things went back to normal. Max understood what was happening and all about his new job. Max realized this was his forever home. He began to calm down and eat, and he showed no signs of sickness. It just goes to show that too much stress can push anyone to the max . . . including your animal companions.

BABY, LEO

Baby Has a Boo-boo

My friend has a beautiful black cat named Baby who developed a tumor on the roof of her mouth. Her veterinarian performed a biopsy and determined the tumor was not cancerous. However, it was apparently uncomfortable for Baby, and it made eating difficult. My friend asked if I could speak with Baby to find out how she was.

I began by asking if it was okay for us to have a conversation. Baby said that it was. I asked her how she was and if she liked her home. She said, "I'm fine. Of course I like it here. This is my home." Baby was very excited to talk to me and wanted to show me all of the stuff around her. She showed me her favorite hiding place: beneath a small round "jumpy" [trampoline]. She wanted to make sure I knew it was a jumpy and not the couch. She then showed me the red and tan colors of the couch that the jumpy stands next to. When she showed me an office desk with lots of papers on it, Baby said, "Our room." My friend said she and Baby spend a lot of time in the office, and then explained that Baby usually hid under the table. Because her other cat, Leo, never goes into the office, it was Baby's special area to be alone with her momma.

Baby told me about a third, gray cat. My friend said that they did not have a third cat or a gray cat. She said she had once taken care of her dad's cat, but that cat was black with gray whiskers, and he had been there before she had adopted Baby and Leo.

Baby was adamant that my friend's father's cat was not the cat she was speaking about. She showed me a glass back door that she liked to look out and from where she could see the gray cat. My friend realized the cat Baby referred to was Mecca, the neighbor's gray cat. Mecca visited their back door daily, but Baby hadn't seen her for a while. Baby wanted to know where Mecca was. Baby showed me another picture of Mecca with her gray fur and white boots. I asked my friend if Mecca had white boots and she confirmed that she did. For some reason Mecca had stopped coming around, and Baby was concerned. I tried to gain a connection with Mecca but was not successful. I did get the feeling that Mecca was fine, however, and hadn't been around while Baby was sick.

My friend told me that Baby was dropped off on a friend's doorstep by the momma cat when Baby was a kitten. Baby was initially raised by her friend's dog, Honey. Baby showed me an image of Honey, a midsize tan dog. My friend confirmed that Honey was a tan Labrador retriever. My friend took both

Baby and Leo in when her friend was unable to take care of them. My friend has had Baby and Leo for just three years, though they are ten and eleven years old respectively.

I turned my attention to Leo to see how things were going with him. Leo was quite grumpy and didn't want to be bothered. He was irritated that I woke him from his nap. He asked, "What do you want?" in a very snide manner. I wanted to make sure he knew his pal Baby was going to be okay. He seemed pleased to hear this information but still wanted to be left alone. I asked if he wanted to come downstairs to be with Baby, and he said, "Not now. In my time." So, I figured I had better let Leo get back to his nap.

I again chatted with Baby and she showed me how beautiful she looked when she groomed herself. I asked her if she would make sure she took her medicine and told her that it would make her momma happy. She said that she would take her medicine and that she didn't want anyone to fuss over her. My friend was happy and relieved and said that Baby was awesome. Baby then chimed in with, "Yes, I am!"

CHARLIE, BOOTS, GABBY

SAM, RIPLEY, KIKO

King Boots

I have some friends who volunteer as fosters for cats for the local rescue shelter. They always have several cats residing at their house and have helped find homes for many more. At one time they had five cats and were looking to bring in an orange tabby named Boots, a really gentle cat that they thought would be able to fit in with any family. But for some reason he was having difficulties with the other cats in the house. My friends asked if I could communicate with Boots and the others to determine why there were problems.

I started with Boots, and he immediately told me, "They don't like me. They always try to trap me. They won't let me have any food or use the potty [litter box]." He said he liked his old house much better than his foster home. I don't think I had ever spoken to a cat that was this concerned and upset. He was trying to fit in, but the other cats wanted no part of him.

I then spoke with Sam, who was known affectionately as the bully of the bunch. Sam was the number-two cat in this male-dominated house. He liked to instigate matters with the other cats and then blame them for what transpired. He even said, "Not my problem . . . it's the other cats" when I asked him about the challenges in the house. It was clear that Sam didn't like Boots and really didn't care much for any of the other cats. He said there were "too many changes" in the house and that there were "too many new cats."

I explained to Sam that the number of cats was only temporary, and they just needed a home until they were adopted. He didn't care and felt that it wasn't his problem that the other cats did not have homes. He said he didn't like Boots touching his stuff and that Boots "smelled." Sam was definitely threatened by Boots—even though Boots had done nothing to provoke it—and Sam wanted to ensure that he kept his place in the hierarchy.

I then spoke to Ripley, one of the females. Ripley wasn't very talkative and really seemed to be lethargic during our brief conversation. She said "I can't be bothered with Boots" and "He's just another male who's doing what males do." She especially didn't like him touching her stuff.

Gabby, the other female, also did not care for Boots. She had enough issues with the other male cats chasing her around. She liked to stay close to her human companion who she called "Mama." She didn't want any cats near her Mama. She finished the conversation by saying, "Boots doesn't belong, and he gets in my stuff."

Charlie is the less-dominant male of the group. He is quiet and shy and doesn't pay much attention to Boots. Charlie feels that he is going to be the odd man out no matter how many new cats are introduced to their home.

Kiko is the alpha male of the group. The rest of the cats don't fear him, but they do respect his wishes and treat him as the king. Kiko didn't care whether Boots stayed or went. However, he didn't like Boots in all of his "stuff." Boots being in their stuff was a consistent concern with this group of cats.

Though I believe that all the cats could have come to a compromise, it was decided by the human companions to find Boots a new home where he would have an easier time adapting. So, once again, Boots packed his bags. It was a fortunate turn of events, however, because Boots found a new home where he was treated like a king, and he never had to worry about bothering another cat's stuff.

If you have a cat that likes to go outdoors, provide a protected area for this purpose. There are pet supply companies that have everything from enclosed cat strollers to chain-linked tunnels that a cat can walk through to sit on the grass. Using one of these options satisfies your cat's need to get out of the house and keeps him safe from cars, predators, and pet theft.

MISCHIEF

Mischief the Jungle Cat

You may remember Mischief from an earlier chapter. I had the opportunity to communicate with her again when her human companion called me about a growth on Mischief's bottom lip that had begun to swell and look infected.

Mischief is always excited to speak to me and show me her new toys. When I visited her, she showed me a small cut on her lower lip and confirmed that it was infected. She showed me how she had cut it by rubbing against a piece of wood. I tried to see the wood she had rubbed against, but I couldn't get a clear picture.

As we continued our guessing game, I remembered that Mischief loved to rub herself against her mommy's plants. I asked my friend whether she thought Mischief might have rubbed against one of her plants and cut her lip. My friend couldn't imagine this was the case since, based on our last conversation, she had put all of her plants on the counter, away from Mischief. About this time, I heard Mischief laughing. She showed me that she got on the counters and rubbed against the plants while her mommy was away. She thought the plants were for "healing," which is why she liked rubbing against them. This was indeed how she had cut her lip. She knew that she was "busted," and I had won the guessing game. It was quite amusing to her.

Mischief then showed me her cat carrier and told me how she really didn't like it. I determined that she associated the carrier with going to the veterinarian. I suggested to my friend that she leave the cat carrier out for a while so Mischief could get used to it and maybe she should even take Mischief on a short, fun trip in it.

Mischief was her normal self, except for the cut on her lip. Whenever she got into trouble, she blamed it on her pal, Angel. She liked being able to sit and listen to the phone conversations her mommy had with friends and family. She also got excited when *she* had a chance to sing and talk on the phone. She even showed me a picture of the cats and Greyhound that belonged to the friend in Albuquerque whom her mommy would talk with on the phone. When I mentioned this to my friend, she wondered how it was possible for Mischief to describe what these animals looked like when she had never met or seen pictures of these pets. I told her that she had spoken with them telepathically and over the phone.

ANTONIO, SHAINA

Antonio Comes
to Town

My friend started a new chapter in her life when she married, bought a house, and got a new job. Though they have no kids together, she and her husband already had a built-in family when they married: three cats and a dog. Everyone seemed to adapt well to the changes and understood each of their roles within the family. Then one day my friend's step-daughter arrived with her cat, Antonio, and their world was turned upside down. Let's just say that

Antonio changed the household dynamics a little bit too much.

Antonio is a beautiful tuxedo cat. To his new human companions, he seemed to be a nice addition to the family. He was always close at hand and initially seemed to play well with the other cats. However, when the human companions weren't looking or when they left the house, Antonio would say, "Let the games begin!" Antonio was the new kid on the block and he had to get a feel for the lay of the land . . . or house in this case. He felt the need to test the other animals to see what he could get away with. He needed to find out who he could bully, scare, or push around—and who he couldn't, so he could befriend them. Antonio was a master at this game. When he caused trouble, he would look around innocently and say, "Who *me*?" Antonio denied all involvement in any trouble that occurred because of his prompting.

No one felt the impact of Antonio like Shaina, who was already an anxious and somewhat nervous cat long before Antonio arrived. She was the number three cat in the house and was afraid that she would drop to number four with Antonio around. Antonio knew he could push Shaina to the limit, and he did. She began hiding under the master bed and would not come out for food or to go potty. Her food dish and litter box were even moved upstairs into the master bedroom, but Shaina remained hidden because she was confused as to why another cat had come into her house and what her new role would be. Shaina's role was to provide the stabilizing energy within the household. She made sure that everyone was feeling good and remained focused on their purposes in life. However, the constant changes and the introduction of a new cat were a little much for her to handle. She hid under the bed to regroup her energy and focus, as well as to keep away from the great disrupter—Antonio!

Even after my visiting with and talking to Shaina a couple of times, she is still confused. Antonio still pushes her buttons and bullies everyone. I'm not sure if there will ever be a compromise between these two. Until Antonio leaves for his new home, Shaina will stay in hiding.

JAKE

Jake's in Charge

Jake, a medium-size Schipperke-Lab mix, rules over the four cats and his human companions in the house where he lives. He's rather small compared to the full-size Labs he plays with, but he thinks he's the biggest dog in the neighborhood. Jake likes being the leader of the cats, and though he sometimes plays a little rough, he never hurts them. Jake has a sensitive soul and a big heart, and he makes a special effort to look out for the cats. He always tries to do what is best, but he sometimes loses his focus. He is a loving boy, but he needs constant reassurance.

Lately Jake has been a little out of sorts. He lives in the same household as Shaina and Antonio from the previous chapter, and the changes have overwhelmed him, causing anxiety. He's confused about the new cat and stepdaughter coming to live with them, and the new blue cat dish and litter pan in the master bedroom. All of the changes have caused Jake to lose focus. He has started doing his "business" inside the house, instead of going outside.

When I visited Jake, I explained to him that all the changes were only temporary and things would get back to normal soon. I communicated to him that he still needed to do his job and look after everyone in the house. I also told him that he needed to do his "business" outside, as he was taught to do. He seemed to accept all of my advice and was glad I came by. I suggested to my friend that she give him a little more reassurance about all the changes and to tell him often that he was a good boy. I also recommended that she let Jake know in advance if there were going to be any additional changes or if she was leaving for a business trip. I also suggested that her husband treat Jake like his personal pal, especially while she was away.

After a couple of weeks passed, things in the household settled down. Jake adjusted to the changes and returned to normal. Everyone, including Jake, had taken my advice and implemented it. Jake was back in charge.

JAKE, SPOT, SAMANTHA

What's Up with All the Spots?

Our pal Jake, the dog, has a tuxedo cat friend named Spot. Jake likes to look out the window to see what Spot is up to. Just the mention of Spot's name gets Jake excited, and he will look out all the windows to try to find her. Not too long ago my friend became concerned because she had not seen Spot around for a while. She asked if I could find out where Spot was. I agreed to help find her.

I began with Jake, who became really excited when I asked him about Spot. He rushed around the house searching for her and looked out each window. I told Jake that Spot hadn't been seen in a while, and I asked if he knew where she was. Jake said, "She's fine. She's alive." I asked if he had seen her and he said, "No. She's on the prowl." I asked him what he meant by Spot being on the prowl. He then showed me a lot of different types of birds. It was obvious that Spot was out bird hunting, a favorite pastime of cats.

Near the end of my chat with Jake, I received an image of a cat in the backyard. At first I assumed it was Spot. Then I discovered the cat in the backyard was a tiger cat, not a tuxedo cat. I focused my attention on the backyard to see if I could visually see a tiger cat, but there wasn't a cat in the backyard. I asked my friend if she had previously had a tiger cat that had transitioned. She confirmed that she had and that the cat's name was also Spot. She had buried him in the backyard.

During the same visit, I also received a strong image of another cat that was not in physical form. I was sure that this cat, too, had transitioned, but I didn't feel that it was buried in the backyard. I asked my friend if she had previously had another cat that had died. She said she had, and she asked me to go upstairs with her to her home office. On the desk in the office was an urn. Beside the urn was a picture of a cat named Samantha, who had come into my friend's life during her first marriage and helped her through some tough times. She explained that Samantha had stayed with her until two months before her second marriage. She had a strong bond with Samantha and deeply appreciated the love and support that she had received from the cat.

I opened a line of communication with Samantha to see how she was. Samantha explained that she was fine and was preparing to come back in the body of a new cat. Her mission here on earth had been to be the "Transition Kitty." She had been here to help my friend through a tough time, and she knew her mission had been fulfilled when my friend was ready to get married and start a new life. Samantha is now preparing to come back to another person to help him/her through a difficult situation and stay until this person is ready to make a positive change in his/her life.

Plan for your pet's future if something should happen to you. Many states allow you to set up trusts for your pets so that they are taken care of in the manner that you desire should you pass away before they do. For more information, visit www.hsus.org/petsinwills or consult with your family attorney.

LUKE

Creepy– Crawlies

My friend has a tiger cat named Luke that has always struggled with his weight, but otherwise, he has been a healthy cat. Recently, I had a chance to spend some dedicated time with Luke.

During the visit, I had a conversation with Luke and provided him with some healing energy. I noticed a tingling sensation each time I moved my hands toward his backside. I spent some time focusing on this area and continued to perform a body scan using Reiki energy to try to determine what was going on. I asked him if he had pain or discomfort in this area. He said he didn't, but I kept feeling the tingling sensation emanating from his backside area.

I focused on this area to try to narrow down the specific spot that could be causing him issues. The tingling intensified when I was near his kidneys. It was more like a "creepy-crawly" feeling, the kind you get when you feel as if bugs are crawling all over your body. I asked my friend if Luke was having any issues with his kidneys. She said she wasn't aware of any issues, and that his latest blood test had not shown any problems.

I suggested she have her veterinarian run some additional blood work on Luke the next time she took him in for a visit. She took my advice, and when the test results came in, some of Luke's blood counts were elevated. The veterinarian thought the elevated counts were an indication that Luke was starting to have kidney problems. The veterinarian suggested changing his diet to include a cat food that focused on helping the kidneys. Of course, the veterinarian had no idea that I had received this same information when I scanned Luke's body during my recent visit.

I have to reiterate that I am not a veterinarian. I also would never ask someone to ignore the advice of an animal's medical caretaker. However, based on what I feel during a scan of the animal's body, I do make recommendations to the human companion as to whether what I receive feels serious enough to seek medical attention or whether it is something minor like pollen affecting an animal's allergies. In either case, I offer Reiki energy healing to the animals during my conversations with them if they are agreeable to it. The energy healing appears to give them a great deal of comfort and helps relieve any stress or anxiety they may be feeling.

CHARLIE, ANTONIO

Sliding On All Fours

Charlie loves to play, and his favorite playmate is a tuxedo cat named Antonio, who you met in an earlier chapter. As a matter of fact, Charlie seems to be the only cat in the four-cat house that gets along with Antonio, probably because they have a similar playful and mischievous energy.

One day my friend came home and noticed that Charlie had developed a slight limp in his back left leg. She had assumed that he must have been playing with Antonio and sprained his leg. After a couple of days, the leg showed signs of improvement. Then, on the third day, it started to flare up again. It had got to the point where Charlie would not eat and only wanted to sleep on the bed. He did manage to get downstairs to the basement to use his litter box, but then he could not make it back up the stairs. My friend had to go down to the basement and carry him back up to the bed. She asked me to have a chat with Charlie to determine what had happened and to see how he felt.

I performed an energy scan of his body and provided him with some energy healing. Charlie showed me what had happened, and my friend's assessment of what she thought had happened was confirmed. Charlie and Antonio had chased each other down the carpeted stairs, and they had landed on the wooden floor in the main room. Antonio had negotiated the landing well, but Charlie had slid across the floor and banged his left hip on the wall, bruising it. Charlie told me that he would be fine. He just needed to rest his injury.

A couple of weeks passed, and Charlie was back to his old self—chasing Antonio.

MADISON

Madison Meets the Bronx

A wonderful lady from City Island, Bronx, New York, contacted me to help her find her missing tiger cat, Madison. Her apartment was located on the fourth floor of a rather large apartment complex, and she saw Madison jump from the window and run off. Madison had never been outside before and did not have a collar or an identification chip. Fortunately, I was contacted immediately following Madison's escape to see if I could make a connection with Madison and convince her to come back home.

Time was of the essence since Madison was unfamiliar with her surroundings and had never been on her own. I had no idea if Madison was injured, or worse. When dealing with lost animals, an early connection is crucial. I knew that the more time that elapsed, the less likely it would be that Madison would return home. Madison was facing a very dangerous situation, and after additional time being on her own, the cat would be more concerned about finding food and shelter than in coming home.

Fortunately, on my first attempt I was able to make contact with Madison, who seemed somewhat confused but in good health. This was amazing considering the height from which she had jumped. She told me she had jumped out the window because she was curious about going outside. However, once she was outside, she was confused about what to do and how to get back inside. She conveyed a strong pressure or compression sensation on my chest. This was a different sensation from what I had previously felt when I dealt with an animal that had experienced heart or chest problems. This was more of a confining sensation, like she was hiding in a small area. Madison confirmed that she was indeed hiding in a warm dry spot and planned to stay there for the night.

The neighbors spotted Madison at the doorstep of the apartment complex the next morning. However, they thought she was a stray since she did not have a collar. Madison could not figure out how to get inside the apartment building, so she left. I was asked to send a message to her requesting that she show up at the doorstep the next morning at 6:00 AM and her momma would be waiting for her. Madison understood what I requested, but she was a little unsure of what 6:00 AM meant. I further explained that she should show up at the doorstep a little before sunrise. She still seemed a bit confused, but she agreed to try. The next morning came and went with no sign of Madison.

I decided to try map dowsing to pinpoint Madison's location. Map dowsing is an excellent way to determine where any lost animal started its journey, where it has been during its time away, and where it may be at that moment. The technique involves taking a large map of the area where the animal was last seen and, using a pendulum, narrowing down its current location. Although it is a long and tedious process, it can nevertheless be highly successful. You can usually narrow down the area to a neighborhood, a street, or an exact location.

As I began to narrow down my search, I learned that Madison had not strayed far from the apartment where she lived. She showed me that she was in a grassy area with a lot of trees and bushes. From looking at the map, I could tell that the front of the apartment building faced the water, and the back part of the building faced a small wooded area. This was the area where Madison was staying. I suggested to her momma that she go to the back door of the apartment building and begin calling out Madison's name. She tried this for most of the day and night but Madison did not turn up.

I further suggested to Madison's momma that she set out a humane trap by the back of the apartment building. I told her momma to make sure that she put some very smelly food in the trap and to cover it with Madison's favorite blanket or towel. The scent would attract Madison, and her blanket would add some protection. All we could do next was wait to see if Madison would appear. Unfortunately, she didn't, and another night went by.

To cover all the bases, I also suggested putting signs up throughout the neighborhood, especially at the local restaurants. In addition, I recommended that she check the local county animal shelters and veterinarians to make sure they didn't have Madison. Fortunately, all of this had already been done.

I continued to map dowse the area to see if I could locate Madison. I made sure I performed the map dowsing once in the morning and once in the evening. I wanted to see if there were any patterns that we could follow. The map dowsing showed me that Madison was on the move most of the day, exploring the area and looking for food. At night, she would come back to the area around the apartment complex.

The next day, I was able to make contact with Madison again. She showed me that someone had fed her and that she was hiding around a house with a basement window and wooden porch. There were several houses in the neighborhood that matched this description, but it helped to narrow down where she was during the day.

Later that day a lady who lived a couple of blocks away contacted Madison's momma. The neighbor said she had seen Madison sunbathing in her backyard. She had fed Madison but assumed she was one of the stray cats who hung around her house. She had noticed that Madison appeared to be well-groomed, but she wasn't wearing a collar. She had not known Madison was lost until she saw one of the posters in the neighborhood.

I continued to map dowse the area and communicate with Madison every day. The results and responses kept coming back the same. I continued to encourage Madison's momma to continue her efforts with the postings, contacting neighbors, and setting the humane trap. Two weeks had passed, and Madison had still not returned.

Madison's momma contacted me and told me about a feral male cat that hung around the apartment building. This cat was quite the bully and was more aggressive when he was on the prowl. Since this was spring, it made matters worse. I told her I would try to communicate with the feral bully cat to see if he would let Madison pass. The feral cat said that he would allow Madison to pass to get to her home, but she needed to do it soon. I communicated this information to Madison, but she seemed a little afraid to commit to this agreement.

One night, the feral cat got trapped in the humane trap. The stinky food was too tempting, and my coaxing him into the cage helped a little as well. The feral male cat was taken away to be neutered, thus leaving the coast clear for Madison to return. I communicated this information to Madison that night. I stayed up most of the night communicating with Madison and convincing her to return home. I was exhausted, but hopeful.

The next morning I received an e-mail from Madison's momma: "MADISON IS HOME!!!!"

Nearly three weeks to the day, Madison's adventure came to an end. Safe and sound, she cuddled into her favorite blanket and was thankful to be home again.

Afterword

The tales listed in this book are in chronological order. As you read from tale to tale, you probably recognized that I initially received the information mainly in words from the animals. As the tales in the book progressed, I received the information from the animals in multiple ways in addition to words, including feelings, smells, tastes, emotions, and images.

Today when I communicate with animals, I continue to receive the information in all of those forms. I have found that the form used depends on the preference of the particular animal with which I am communicating.

It is my hope that these tales have given you insight into the minds of animals and helped you realize how intelligent and special they are. Always remember to open your mind and heart to these beautiful creatures because every animal has a tale.

More Tips from Tim

I thought it would be helpful to provide some more tips about animals that I have learned over the years. I hope that they are useful to you and your pet(s).

1. If you leave the house for any reason, tell your pet(s) where you are going, when you will return, and what job you would like them to do while you are gone. I always tell my dogs that I'm going to run an errand, when I will be back (e.g., two hours, around dinner, etc.), and I need them to take a nap and be good boys while I'm

gone. This tends to relieve their anxiety about me being gone.

2. Animals like routines. If their routine is going to change for a day or longer, tell them what to expect. For example, if you are going to have to work late for a couple of weeks, tell your pet. This will help to ward off any unwanted behavior that it may exhibit as its way of protesting the change to its routines.

3. If your animal has seizures, ask your vet to test it for food allergies. One of our dogs began to have seizures shortly after we brought him home from the shelter. We had our veterinarian perform a comprehensive allergy test and discovered that he had many allergies, including chicken and rice, which were both in the food we were feeding him. The company that provided the results from the allergy test also provided a list of foods (canned and dry) and treats that he would not be allergic to. We switched his food, and he hasn't had another seizure. Food allergies may not always be the cause of seizures, but it is worth investigating.

4. Spay or neuter your pet. Millions of animals in rescue shelters are euthanized each year because there aren't enough homes for all of them. Spaying and neutering your pet will help put an end to the pet overpopulation problem. In addition, there are several additional health benefits to an animal being spayed/neutered that your veterinarian can tell you about.

5. Post the Animal Poison Control twenty-four-hour hotline number (1-800-548-2423) near your phone.

6. Prepare for disasters. Make sure you have a plan in place in the event of a hurricane, tornado, fire, or flood.

7. If you are planning on vacationing with your pet, find out ahead of time if the place where you will be staying accepts pets and what requirements it has about pets being on the premises (e.g., leash laws, cleanup requirements, pet deposits, etc.).

8. If you are planning on vacationing without your pet, investigate the facility where you will be boarding your pet. Is it clean? Do the

animals in its care look happy? Are there areas for the animals to play alone or with other animals their own size? What would they do if your animal has a medical problem while you are away? Are the facility hours convenient for when you need to drop off and pick up your pet? Does the facility require proof of current vaccination records prior to boarding the animals?

9. Teach children the proper way to approach an unfamiliar animal. This includes asking the owner's permission to pet the animal. Some animals are not used to children and can react adversely if approached too quickly.

10. An alternative to boarding your animal(s) when you are on vacation is to have someone from a pet-sitting company come into your home and stay with your pet(s). In my opinion, and based on my own experience with my pets, this option is less stressful on the animal because it gets to remain in familiar surroundings while you are gone. If you choose to go this route, ask for referrals from the company's current customers, make sure the company is

licensed and insured, meet the person who will be watching your pet, and see how the person interacts with your pet(s). Finally, ask if the pet-sitting company is part of any national pet-sitting association (e.g., National Association of Pet Sitters [NAPS]). Also remember to leave detailed instructions with the pet sitter about how to handle each of your pet(s), as well as your contact information and what the sitter is to do if there is a medical emergency while you are away.

If you have any tips about animals that you would like to see printed in a future publication or on the Wagging Tales Web site, www.wagging-tales.com, please e-mail me at timlink@wagging-tales.com.

TIM

About the Author

Tim Link is president and CEO of Link's Wagging Tales, Inc., and he is a practicing animal communicator and Reiki energy healer for animals. He is a featured expert on the *Atlanta Journal-Constitution*'s AJCpets.com Web site and volunteers as the president of the Humane Society of Forsyth County (a no-kill shelter).

Tim grew up in Richmond, Indiana. He married his high school sweetheart, Kim, and graduated from Ball State University with a Bachelor of Science degree. After graduation, he built a successful twenty-plus-year career in sales management for the telecommunications industry, earning numerous awards and promotions for his achievements.

In February 2004, Tim learned (with great surprise) that he could communicate telepathically with animals. Until then, he had no idea he had this ability. Initially, he never intended to let many people know about this newfound gift. He practiced with his own pets and those of his family and close friends, as well as those boarded at the local rescue shelter. As he continued to practice on more and more animals, his gift continued to grow stronger. One day, one of the volunteers at the local rescue shelter "outed" him and the gift that he had by asking him to help one of her friends with her pet.

After much contemplation, he decided to embrace this gift and this new way of helping all types of animals and their human companions as a profession.

Tim has helped many animals in many situations and continues to do so on a daily basis.

More information about Tim and the services he provides can be found on his Web site, www.wagging-tales.com, or by e-mailing him at timlink@wagging-tales.com.